Talking to Ghosts

Selected Poems 1983 - 1992

Philip Gardner

BREAKWATER
100 Water Street
P.O. Box 2188
St. John's, NF
A1C 6E6

The Publisher gratefully acknowledges the financial support of the Canada Council, which has helped make this publication possible.

The Publisher acknowledges the financial support of the Cultural Affairs Division of the Department of Municipal and Provincial Affairs, Government of Newfoundland and Labrador, which has helped make this publication possible.

Cover painting: "There is nothing left of the sea but its sound" by Gerald Squires.
Author photo: John Bourne

Canadian Cataloguing in Publication Data
Gardner, Philip.

Talking to ghosts

Poems.
ISBN 1-55081-077-4

I. Title

PS8563.A63T35 1993   C811'.54   C93-098719-5
PR9199.3.G37T35 1993

Copyright © 1993 Philip Gardner

ALL RIGHTS RESERVED. No part of this work covered by copyrights hereon may be reproduced or used in any form or by any means—graphic, electronic or mechanical—without the prior written permission of the publisher. Any request for photocopying, recording, taping or information storage and retrieval systems of any part of this book shall be directed in writing to the Canadian Reprography Collective, 379 Adelaide Street West, Suite M1, Toronto, Ontario, M5W 1S5.

Printed in Canada

Acknowledgements

Some of these poems have appeared in the following magazines and anthologies:

Banked Fires: An Anthology of Newfoundland Poetry
Critical Survey
Dalhousie Review
KM 80: A Birthday Album for Kenneth Muir
Newfoundland Quarterly
TickleAce

Contents

Waiting on Christmas Sunday 7
Woodside Ferry 8
Reading 'Spain' to the Students 9
Funerals 10
Reposing 11
78°S 12
For Earle Birney in St. John's 13
Walberswick Pier Head, 1888 14
Spelsbury House 15
Winter View of Liverpool Cathedral 16
Piano Quintet 17
Night Walk 18
March 31, 1992 18
Archbishop 19
For Percy 20
Intensive Care 22
The Target 23
Blundellsands, 1985 24
Tyringham 25
Oak Bay 26
White Point, Trinity Bay 28
Lux Aeterna 30
11 November, 1983 32
Fen Ditton 33
Kurenai Maru 34
31 35
For Hanna, 1944 35
Morning Recess 36

Memorial Service	37
Resurrection, 1987	38
351	40
Wirral	41
Thor's Rock	42
First of December	43
1895	44
Old Haymarket, 1955	45
30 September 1988	46
Mountains	48
Four Mile Point	49
For Oscar in Easter Week	50
Indian Meal Line	51
In Memory of Colonel Robert Shaw	52
Ghosts	53
Sunday Morning, Paris	54
The Long Valley	55
Revisiting	56
Tanglewood, 1991	58
Levelling	60
Elegy for William Mathias	61
Palm Sunday, Thornton	62
Creation	63

Waiting on Christmas Sunday

First it was light, rushing through stained-glass saints
To splinter on stone; all through the morning
The sun set fire to the arches.

Then it was wind: the great church on its ledge
High above the harbour, a dry-docked ship,
Shook and shivered its timbers

Round sermon, wine, recessional of organ,
Chasuble and mitre. The heavy doors
Banged to and fro, flew open

On a clean exhilaration of mid-day,
Crushed ice of pavements, freezing blue of sky
Where, over the dull red brick

Of the Deanery, a hefted seagull sailed
Slowly, and a weightless crumple of plastic
Bowled above gable and roof

To lodge in wiry branches. There was no spire
To measure the sky's racing to the east,
But far down the hill white waves

Whipped across cold green water. The streets were empty.
I trod the half-compact, half-melting snow,
Or leaned my head on the hard

Arch of the locked cathedral: a long half-hour
On a knife-edge, at the middle of the world, alone
With the white heat of Christmas.

Woodside Ferry

Mist on the Southside Hills. My car door opens
On a rumour of damp air
Blown from the harbour, the salt-and-oily smell
Of ships and water. How many years
Since crossing the Mersey! *Woodchurch* and *Hinderton*
Pushing aside the mile-wide river
On blue weekends, or grey; the cry of sea-gulls
Over the mast-head lamps, the sharp salt wind
Across the open upper deck, the squat
Roped wooden seats; the shiver
As Liver Building and cathedral rose
Behind, and the brick ramparts of the Wirral
Grew higher, nearer. Treading a foam of water,
The ferry bumped its rubber fenders
As men in dark-blue jerseys
Shouted and threw their ropes. And then the swivel
Of metal, the shuddering drop of gang-planks,
The rush to be first off, the pounding feet
Up the steep, echoing ramp
To air, and the blue buses
Delivering the world.
                    Thirty-odd years
Of water widening, more and more opaque,
Mersey and Irish Sea and cold Atlantic.

Reading 'Spain' to the Students

(for Kenneth Muir)

Firmly you opened out
The same red covers, fading now,
You'd paid a shilling for at thirty
To go to *Medical Aid for Spain*,
And spoke. You were his generation,
And they, spare transatlantic faces,
Too young to know the pulse of war.

I closed my eyes, hearing your deep voice dig
With the edge of his cool phrases
Caverns of resonance, unimagined
Echoes. Younger myself, I couldn't
Have read like that.
                    Absorbed in sound, I didn't
Catch where the poem skidded
For you out of marmoreal eloquence
Into the past, re-lived; but suddenly heard
The emotion rising in your throat
Too harsh to quell, and snapped awake to see
His words your own, indomitable blue eyes
Leaking the angry
Red of tears. Beyond our shock, they gazed
Inward, further and further, into the unanswering
Abysses of history, reaching out
For the irretrievable hands, the vanished voices.

Funerals

Words over polished wood;
Songs to distract
Blank eyes from silence, glued
To the brute fact.

Urned ash; mouldering bone;
Hacked rock, wet clay;
Tilted albums of stone
Wearing away.

Garbage, pet after pet
On dumps tossed out;
Shriek of speed to forget
The seagulls' shout.

Carcases, final ends;
The city's edges
Where sudden dark descends;
Foundering ledges.

Overgrown sidings; choke
Of cyanide, hissing;
The huge impalpable smoke
Of the missing.

Extinctions out of sight;
On thin, grey shales
Under Antarctic white,
Bleak windrows of whales.

Reposing

(in memory of Ron Seary, 1908-1984)

Your door open, as always.
A glow from table-lamps,
Over-sized sofas, *Time*
And *People* on the coffee-table:
The impersonal comfort
Of an office waiting-room,

And your name above the lintel
Just as for fifty years
Of Rhodes, Baghdad, Memorial:
DR. E.R. SEARY. But the silence
Presses; the white-on-black
Lettering could as well spell out

TENDERLOIN STEAK SANDWICH
$4.95. Inside your final
And biggest office there's an empty
Sofa, the florid easel
Of a botany lesson, and your desk's
On wheels: a deaf mahogany

Casket, antiqued with chrome,
Shut fast. All that shows
Is a last brass plate (name, age)
And the folds of a scarlet and rose
Hood. I wanted to see you,
But for once, for ever, you're out.

78°S

At Hut Point
Everything is silent.

Antarctic light
Narrows through double-glazed
Lenses of windows
On a still life
Of wood and metal:

An upended tin
— Orange, gold, royal blue —
Of Huntley & Palmer's
Superior 'Captain' Biscuits;
Split peas; a 4lb.
Discoloured paper bag
(Tate & Lyle, Liverpool)
Of cube sugar;
A box of Special
Dog Biscuits, big as a coffin
— Vida, and Osman,
Tresor, Krisarovitsa;
A yellowing crate
(Its two hemp handles
Waiting to be lifted)
Of 'Homelight' Lamp Oil;
A spirit stove.

I need not name the men

Gone into the cold
For seventy-two years,
Leaving their age
Stopped here like a watch
In brands and boxes:
The dry biscuits, the lumps
Of sugar you could still
Crunch, listening for them
Against wind and time;

The hardly-clouded
Oil you could still burn.

For Earle Birney in St. John's

Rangy old poet, loping in
From winter with a carpet-bag
Of records, volumes;

Needing no introduction, gently
Whispering, fluting, every word
Distinct and lingering;

A compass rose
Of winds and harbours,
Longings and curiosities

Unquenched; your beard as crisp as snow,
Your pink and white-wisped skull
Innocent as a babe's again;

Eyes crinkled with experience
— War, and death, and love —
And smiling up at us;

Eighty this year, still trying
Everything on, still stretching out
To mythical dimensions;

Lays of a last
Wandering minstrel, wreathed
In the spring leis of our applause.

Walberswick Pier Head, 1888

Morning and freshening wind
Blow in from Holland; points of light
Dance on the grey-blue water,
The North Sea narrowing to its waist
From Walberswick to Zandvoort.
The horizon quickens
To a stroke of white; dark smudges
Are sails of ocean-going barges,
Becalmed inside the picture, tugging
Slowly towards its margin, bearing down
Over sunk Dunwich to the Naze, and London.

Was it the light that caught him,
The ever-shifting flecks, the tanned
Sandy foreshore, shadows leaning back
From wooden groyne and bollard?
It leaps at you, his oils
Refract the invisible sun
Into a rainbow, an expectancy
Vibrant here for ever.

                        But Wilson Steer
Was 28: the summer morning light
Throws back the shadows of two girls
In long pink dresses, scarlet sashes
Flowing in the wind. The near one's hair
Streams down her shoulders, her black stockings
Brace on the sand, her face
Gazes without features to the east.
Nearly a century later
We watch her watching, as the rise
Of sunlight takes the prow of her straw hat
Shaped like a paper boat: someone he loved,
Perhaps, his nervous brush running to catch her
Sailing away into the future,
Her pink dress blown behind her like a flag.

Spelsbury House

(for James and Belinda Price)

Yew trees and pale
Oxfordshire stone; all day the Evenlode
Moved like slow glass, unseen, beyond
Lawn green, reed green, hedge green, the hidden
Edge of the stretching garden, struck
Still under the spell of perfect
August. All the afternoon
The high sun's ball of blinding steel
Leaned, slanted, curved along and down
Its thin invisible groove across
Burnished blue emptiness. The quiet
Relentlessness of heat translated
Skin into light; the sounds of summer
Echoed absorbed within the ear:
Plock of a tennis ball, transparent
Splash of blue water in a pool, the cool
Long soporific call across the poplars
Of wood-pigeons.
                          All day the great
Ringed eyes of dusty orange butterflies
Folded and opened, hovering
On purple buddleia. The church tower
Sat square, unaltering, framed in trees:
Dark green, pale gold. The distance
Of Wychwood shaded into smoke of late
Light, and the Evenlode flowed slowly
Under the far field's slope of sun.

Winter View of Liverpool Cathedral

(for Kenneth Muir)

Three-quarters of a century
In stone! A deep blue winter sky
Above St. James's Cemetery,
Delicate skeletons of trees,
And shadows on untrodden snow
Converging on that monument
To time, as if huge figures stood
Outside the picture, looking in
From far away. The single park
Bench in the centre ground is bare.

Such stillness! But I cannot feel
The bracing edge of cold, or hear
Wind's dry enchantment in the trees,
Or watch that great white cloud go by
High as the massive tower, and leave
Its sandstone brighter on the blue.
No thousand pipes behind the tall
Arches of sombre ruby glass
Salvo their Christmas music out
To thin like smoke through morning air.

Instead, my eye is carried back
Down silent avenues of snow;
Birch trees and obelisks recede
Like years, towards some unseen point
Where I began. The ghosts reach out
To touch me as I pass, but hide
Their faces when I look: too vague,
Too far for proper names by now,
Too many! Only, high above,
The calm cathedral never fades:

A transept less, an arch, a bay
As I diminish, but alive
When I am lost. It grows with me
Year upon year as I return
Out of the picture, stand, look back
And up. How chancel, nave and tower
Collect inscrutable in stone
All that my human memory
Has stored, blurred and forgotten: time
Present, still there when I am dead.

Piano Quintet

Brahms never saw the twentieth century in.
He died in 1897 — cancer
Of the liver (all those years of strong
Coffee!), a bare month after
Hiding behind the velvet curtains
Of his box, to mute Vienna's valedictions
Applauding his Fourth Symphony.
                                                  A gruff
Old bachelor of fixed habits
Living in rented rooms, did he think,
Dying, of Clara, gone the year before,
And feel a last leap through his muscles
Of a young man's passion, hearing
The strings still signalling to her, and his great
Hands striking fire from the flint keys?

Night Walk

The freight train's great bright eye
Bores through the darkness, blinding;
Below, the river rushes,
Swollen with melt; above,
The clouds move, in the same fresh wind
That nips our ears, so purposefully
Eastward; they separate, and show
Space, almost stars. Beneath our feet,
Hard snow-crust, fissuring, the first
Reassurance of pavement. Soon
The throbbing cab, long-muzzled un-
derneath the bridge, will jolt and start
To pull its load slowly five hundred
Narrow miles west, and spring will blow
To free imprisoned green.

March 31, 1992

The last traces of snow
Thin from the fawn fields.
The worst winter will go,
Time says, as the ice age yields
To another spring, and shields
Melt from the heart. Below

That five-month carapace
We've had to see and suffer
— Indurations of ice,
Our skins worn daily rougher —
Something has begged to differ
And bursts up now as grass

And hope again, and words
Stirring to re-express
What we'd forgotten. Birds
Cluster in tall bare trees
And suddenly sing, and less
Is more, I sing in thirds.

Archbishop

Always the same walk, a measured
Cycle of prayer; the quiet figure
In black, his coat like a soutane,
Moving with careful even-ness
Along the pavement from St. Patrick's
Past park and brewery and drug-store
Under the loom of hills. A quarter
Of a mile? The time it takes to say
A decade of Hail Marys? Eyes
Rarely look up; his feet (today
In overshoes against late snow)
Tick like a rosary.
                        His rimless
Spectacles once blinked a pale
Smile as I passed him, quicker. I
Smiled back: at some retired old priest,
I thought, waiting it out.

                            But wasn't he
The one who shook my hand, and many,
Hand after hand on New Year's Day
A decade back, at home with gleaming
Silver and wood? He murmured something
To everyone, the gentle smile
Was broader, the kind face had more
Flesh on it then, the black soutane
Was silk, lit up with crimson.
                                   Now
There's just a simple room, a bed,
A crucifix on a white wall
To look at; and, on civil days,
An old man's constitutional —
The introspective, counted yards
Along one street, and back again,
As all life's superfluity
Melts from the bone, and more than man
Grows nearer, clearer, smiles, and speaks.

For Percy

The 'great white': that was what we called you —
A yellow-eyed, firm, furry bundle.
I used to pick you up, and hold you
To watch the silent, big flakes trundle

Down your reflection. 'Look, out there',
I'd whisper in your neck's thick pile,
'It's snowing cats'. You'd purr and stare
At a sky full of Percys, while

I stroked the windfall cat who'd tumbled
Immaculately from the dark
Like luck into our arms, who'd stumbled
From Donovans Industrial Park

Into a life. How little later
Your perfect upward springs, to land
On me, or window-high, to chatter
At birds! (You couldn't understand

Why, when you knocked the fireguard over
And caught your sole one, I should praise
Your skill, then free it. I saw you hover
So tensely by the hearth for days.)

Two Christmases, a year, you made
The house more ours for being yours.
You liked to juggle pens, you played
With lobbed-up foil, relaxed blunt paws

On each semester's heap of script;
And, evenings when I fondly thought
I'd settled down, you looked, and leapt
Up to the safety of my shirt

And burrowed, sucking for dear life
Wetter and wider; then you'd curl
In sleep, or like a risen loaf
Bask purring on the orange stool.

Floors, sofa, trees became as thrones
And blossomed in your calm content.
I came home from the sticks and stones
And you were there. It all seemed meant.

Then, suddenly, your magazine
Of lovely postures shrank to these:
Monotonies of rest, and then
Slow walks to rest elsewhere, to ease

Something that puzzled you inside
And wouldn't go. They cut a square
Of warm fur from your neck for blood
That answered your pale yellow stare

At nothing. Now I pick the fine
Hairs of your moulted life, and see
No cat like Percy fall again
Out of this white and wintry sky.

I thought you'd help to see me through.
You would have done so much. Instead,
There was nothing we could do for you.
I'm forty-nine, and you are dead.

Intensive Care

(for Philip Larkin)

Your subject, of course.
The intra-venous drip
Dropping, the heart-beat
Hiccuping like a slow
Earth-worm across the watched
Hospital speed-trap —

Who else could give these last
Mechanical mensurations
Human meaning? What
Other poet could enter
The individual vein,
Register the elations

That are blanching, now,
Into the universal
Remoteness far beyond
Disappointment? You knew
What was coming to us —
Shrinkage, dispersal —

But to think of you going
Leaves me at a loss,
Meeting your direct look
On the Corporation pier
As the ferry gets up steam
To move off, and cross

Over to New Holland,
And thinking of you flat
On a ward bed, the bright
Ball of your heart bouncing
Across a small screen, less
And less; a blink; then not.

The Target

No stopping. Tarmac thumping past
At thirty yards a second. Just
Time to register it, to rush

Through 'What's that?', 'Isn't it a shame',
And then: 'O God', the sweat
Cold-beading, the accessory hands

Taut on the wheel. Not something off
The back of a lorry, but a dog
Sprawled in the fast lane, lying

Not dead, the muscles suddenly
Shuddering, the white teeth in the lifting
Head of a young black Labrador

Opening against our traffic, a quick
High howl I caught through closed glass, passing
In the next lane. What likely hope

From the police car stopped ahead,
Then small behind, on the hard shoulder?
What chance to check the mindless race

You'd somehow wandered into, trailing
Someone's red ribbon round your neck
Until you glanced against a blur

That dared not brake or veer, that slammed you
Down among hurtling metal? How much
Longer, how many twitches, eyes

Reflecting Western Avenue's
Bewilderment of bright, late sun
Before the next car in a hurry

Finished you off? My useless words
Press in upon that vacuum, tense
Round the still second before death.

Blundellsands, 1985

Each step distinct on concrete:
A quiet walk, alone,
Down to the shore, before
Breakfast in the hushed hotel.
It's eight o'clock. The silver-
grey of a train to Southport
Slides past the corner of my eye.

I lived here, sixteen years ago.
The high house rises; Warren Road
Leads nowhere. There's the school
My small son trotted to each morning,
Private, recessed. No wind,
Only the murmur of a tractor
Transferring sand, and an enormous

Still astonishment of sky
Roofing the estuary. I stop
At a steel rail, as if I'd walked
Into the river's sleep: a swan-
shaped cloud, arrested, edged with light,
Over the distant, leaping-near
Towers of the city; and a gleam

Throwing New Brighton's shallow
Dome like a ball towards my hand,
Infallible as childhood. Ridged
Sand, flat water, waiting
As if I dreamed them; and, far out,
Small as a bird, a cycle's
Slow wheels, poised between sea and land.

Tyringham

(for Humphrey)

'1799' it said on the house
In the Tyringham valley. The house was made of stone
Painted white to look like wood — or was it really
Brick painted white? No sooner seen than flown

A hundred yards behind on that country road
Without a number, running south-east between
Lee and Otis. I write these lines to remember
A cool Colonial house above browny-green

Un-manicured meadows. Beyond the fence and the cows
Grazing by scrubby bushes, those rolling hills
Of no particular height were the real Berkshires,
But only we were looking, and those whose skills

Deserved the valley, since 1754
— White wood in the village — and 1799
Going one better in brick. They had the knowledge
Where was Lost Farm. We passed and missed the sign.

Oak Bay

(for Joan Ryan)

Still light at nine; still water lapping in
        From Cattle Point to Turkey Head;
Still warm; above, a pale thin slice of moon
        And glimmering mosaic of cloud.

We listened to the quiet. Something breathed
        Behind the incompletely shut
Boards of Marineland: something moved and seethed
        Across a square of pool, went phut

Into the air, exhaled a plume like steam
        That spoke to us. We saw a fin
Rise like a periscope, and the wet gleam
        Of a black back curve out, then in.

An orca, circling; two; how many more?
        It was a privilege to see
That strangeness, all for nothing, none to roar;
        A guilt, too, knowing them not free

But only resting, between shows. Their sound
        Showered up like sighing. Round we walked
And down the muted entrance gang-plank, leaned
        With a few others over dark

Water, a polystyrene ledge of ice
        That mocked the real thing. Then, as if
Allowed that forecourt space to advertise
        How, for a fee, they'd strut their stuff,

The seals swam in, six in that narrow space
    Sliding and turning, rounded, sleek,
Bobbing up whiskered heads like dogs. Wet eyes
    Held ours, appraised. They did not speak,

But suddenly — who copied whom? — pulled out
    Great polished bodies, spotted, plain,
On to that artificial shelf, off-white,
    And lying, made it ice again

Such as they'd known once, somewhere. As we watched,
    They reared on awkward flippers, posed
And seemed to bask a moment; then were snatched
    By instinct in, down, under, cruised

Forward and back, deep shadows, one by one
    Ducking the underwater wall
To leave us twilit, settling for their own
    Element, shrunken: orca, seal.

White Point, Trinity Bay

A Group of Seven lake:
Pale green, grey rock —
Background receding into wilderness,
Foreground of ripple-less water
And floating mist

At noon. A perfect place
There at the end of a green road,
Waiting for us to find it.
Deserted; not a sound or movement.
And yet, what was that flat

Door, like a long white stepping-stone
From rocks to water?
Whose were the bluejeans lying on it
As if left out to dry, those pale
Blue Y-fronts in the bushes?

No sign at all, no break
On still primeval calm: a boy
Sunk without trace. And where was she,
The slender lady of the lake,
Vapourised from her pink

Sneakers and faded peach
Towelling knickers? What UFO
Spirited them up? What local passion
(Twin Bonaventures far away
Over the hill a steeple looked from)

Had reached its premature naked climax
By lapping water, left us speechless
As mist at last cleared from the blue
Pond, the pre-Cambrian half-bald hills,
And from the sudden sea

Behind our backs? We sat there
On green, drank in a world of calm,
Pondered white stumps of old foundations,
Hay in a sheepfold, but no sheep,
Rock teeth of headlands, islands trending

Emptily south, a distant sigh
Of long-abandoned settlement
Under a hot blue silent sky.

Lux Aeterna

(for William Mathias)

You must have been in Whitland that late summer
I was in Laugharne. Just fifteen miles away
By Western Welsh, you tinkered at your music
Towards an Aberystwyth First; while I,
Lodged in that local copper's upstairs room,
Ticked off the hourly buses to Pendine
And thought of Dylan Thomas, two years dead,
And of my Part One Essay — Cambridge, but

Only a Lower Second. Caitlin rolled
Furiously over and over on the grass
Next to the Boathouse, in the smallest shorts
I'd ever seen, pink gingham, frilly-edged,
Wrestling with some suave teak-faced macho man
She'd taken a post-prandial scunner to.
I tried to look away from butter hair
And kicking legs. That night her brusque 'Amuse us'

Struck me stone-dumb. But it was Caitlin read
My first real poem, rubbed from old grey stone
And bluebells and gold-glowing organ-loft
At Brecon Cathedral. 'Yes, a feel for words' —
Something like that. Nothing, of course, like Dylan,
Whose ghost I struggled after up Sir John's
Sweltering hill: I never reached the top
For flies, never looked down to see the Taf

Glittering across the mud-flats. Just a week
I stayed there. One wet day I took the bus
To Tenby, Pembroke, Pembroke Dock; then back
By Haverfordwest, trundling in rinsed-out light
Through Whitland. I was nineteen-plus, and you
Near twenty-one, on vacation, somewhere in
Those unremarkable houses, filling staves
With notes I couldn't match, an ear half-cocked

For 'woman trouble', the up-rising call
To dinner on the table. Thirty years
Later, your mother's dead, those fifteen miles
Have rippled out to thousands, and I listen
To what the grown son wrote her. Yes, we're both
Professors now; but how can words of mine
Equal your music's swirl of ghostly bells
Around her memory, Whitland once, and Laugharne?

11 November, 1983

It was as if I'd parachuted in
Silently from the future; not
Stepped off the platform of the first
28 bus, and walked down Violet Road
Listening to the echoes of my steps
In Sunday morning calm. A sign
On palings by the metal railway bridge
Told me again that this was AKENSIDE STREET,

BOOTLE. Grass sprouted out like tufts of hair
Between the dark blue bricks above my head,
Alert. I waited. Did I hear a boy
Come running down steep steps out of the past
To duck the pavement hand-rail, straighten up
On cobbles? Tarmac now. Two railway lines
No longer crossed here: open blue
Where once the LMS's high, oblique

Viaduct spanned the electric. No dark arch,
No cinder path beneath, no nine-year-old
Dashing through shadows, but a green
Rise to a grassy clump, and over all
Wide sky. I seemed to stand there out of time
At some beginning of the world,
Where something still, earlier than myself,
Waited in total silence to be found.

Fen Ditton

All afternoon the small bird lay
Just opposite the glassed front porch
Under a grass-encircled bush.
Surely it hadn't tried to fly?
Perhaps an unintended push
Tumbled its feathers from the high

Nest in the guttering. Now it lay
Almost too small to see; not quite;
As still as lead, except its throat
Opening, closing emptily.
Rasping on gravel, the mower's bite,
Just missing it, had focused me

Inexorably on it. What
To do? Attempting not to know,
I mowed, then raked. But just below,
There it still was. I couldn't put
It back, and how on earth to show
Where to its mother? And the cat —

I'd seen what Charlotte did to birds:
The pounce, the flurry, the escape
Of tiny blood, the sickled leap,
The gape of hopeless vocal chords,
The moulting shuttlecock tossed up
Then crunched to nothing but last words

Of silent claws. In summer sleep
The shorn green garden stretched. How long,
Cat or starvation? All was wrong.
With gloves on, like a bottle cap
I twisted off its head, and flung
The body on the compost heap.

Kurenai Maru

Late afternoon in crisp
October; wine-dark waves
Curdling to foam below
An onward-nudging bow.
Like levitated sheaves
Clouds in procession drift

Far off and white behind
A near, straight head that light
Slants down to slice in two
Against pale turquoise blue
Of sky: one side burned bright,
The other black and blind.

The head is mine, borne on
Inexorably west
Between humped mountains (right)
And (left) the golden-white
Sandspit and rocky crest
Lifting its pines to sun.

Getting towards four-thirty,
When Jobst von Einem took
This *vergissmeinnicht* shot
Far down the widening slot
Of Inland Sea. I look
At him 'near Imabari',

An hour away, perhaps,
From Matsuyama ('pine
Mountain'), where I got off.
All past now, just the stuff
Of dreams. Of him, no sign.
I look across the lapse

Of thirty years at me,
Eyes screwed up not at strong
Sunlight, short-sighted in
Spectacles, but the spin
Of years away, the long
Rifling of history.

31

Light shimmered downwards slowly, genuine gold
Behind green currency of trees. Why then,
Happily tilted back, and looking through,
Should I so suddenly remember you,
A quarter-century gone, betrayed by men,
And think of your young poems, now so old,

Sylvia? Would you have liked it if you'd lived
Beyond that inhalation of cold gas —
Finding the one you'd loved become a name
To reckon with? Are you content with fame
Six feet below this summer waving? Was
Silence the treasure only you conceived?

For Hanna, 1944

The snow matched your blouse.
Four well-spaced bullets
Soaked both in rose,
And you fell, in slow motion,

Silently into death
In the Conti prison —
Empty now, except
For guards; Roszsa; Simon;

The officer; his four
Men, obeying orders;
And you on that floor
Of snow, smiling, beyond them.

Morning Recess

(for Kathryn)

I timed it wrong. Did something time it right?
All I expected was tarmac, ranks of cars,
Perhaps some winning number. Instead, such light
Out of warm blue, children at play on bars
Of jungle gyms, swarming in clothes so bright

It could have been the summer again. Such sliding
Down helter-skelters, such happy noise to match
That Brahms allegro. Parking, not quite hiding
Behind the visor, I settled down to watch;
Then saw dark hair, a grey coat, someone guarding

That grassy mound, those children at their untrained
Music and movement. She too moved about,
Serenely. Was it her shoulder-bag that pained,
Its white just not a metronome on taut
Long straps? Was it her slenderness? I strained

Across the gap neither of us could cross
As cello, then piano and full strings spun
Out their slow notes of longing and of loss,
And under the late miraculous autumn sun
Knew she was you, that distantly turning face

That wouldn't focus. As the tears ran down,
The school bell sharply rang, calling them back
Like birds unsettled. Their flickers blurred my screen,
Filled the held door. The warm air blew your mac
Open, then shut, far off across the green.

Memorial Service

(i.m. Norman Nicholson)

You wrapped your town around you, and that room
Over the Gents' Outfitters your father ran,
Warm with reflected glory. Both of mine
Unravel, disperse, unechoing. Yet Millom

At rising three holds no more than St. John's
Near midnight, now; except that plot of ground
Marked 'Of this parish', where you might be found
Still, perhaps risen. Trinity XIII

Already brings its false dawn to the brink
Of Black Combe, Wrynose, Hard Knott. In Carlisle
(You'd say it Carlisle, if you could), a pile
Of red truncated sandstone starts to blink

Wearily awake. Some time today (tomorrow
From this far off across the sea you saw
Blazing with promise) copes and suits will pour
Words out to speed you, bring you back, turn sorrow

Into a sort of victory, as the light
Smashes as clear as Cartmel through 'the finest
Decorated window in England', and the shiniest
Gold-painted stars gleam from the holy height

Of the blue waggon roof. They owe you that,
Assuming you can hear it. I've not been
Back so far north, inside that noble ruin,
For the three decades since an undergraduate

Read out a choice of long-forgotten verse
For train fare and hotel and a pale blue
Enormous crackling five-pound note that you
Conjured from a Society the years

Have buried too. Where's Thomas Bloomer gone,
The bishop with the funny name? That joke
Boomerangs back towards me through time's smoke,
Norman, and chars in cold September sun.

Resurrection, 1987

Crusader castles rose
Twenty-five miles beyond
The central plain's dead ground.
Afternoons off, we'd gaze
Past wire through quivering haze
Till eyes, enlarging, found

This speck or that, too far
To reach, up-rearing high
Against a vibrant sky
On fretted jets of bare
Granite, above white shore
And endless summer sea.

The trembling distance beckoned
Through windows, as we sat
Cool in the Wivis hut.
Morse-concentration slackened,
We dreamed as Mahler's Second
Revolved at seventy-eight

And wound us in. Each side
Dropped hard, then with a hiss
Ushered us into peace.
Perhaps a whispered word
Would pass, or Carol glide
Smiling, and leave the keys.

Just two, or three at most,
Listening there, as sound
And vision wrapped around
Each other. Which came first?
Castles, or music? Missed,
Did stone speak? Or a wand

Weave shimmering shapes like paint
A year's heat dried to ru-
ined legends, poised on blue:
Dizzy Kantara, Saint
Hilarion, worn-down flint
Of Buffavento? Now,

Across dead ground no eyes
Peer through the haze, there's no
Dim hut. But Mahler's Two
Rebuilds: on listened skies
Crusader castles rise,
Twenty-eight years ago.

351

You only went to Chesterfield, alas,
Unparalleled. You read a music score —
Some "Nocturne" — while the National Express
Idled in early Drummer Street, and more
Problems got on. My ticket was a mess.
"It's going to be that sort of day", he swore,

The harassed pint-sized driver. You looked round,
And caught my eye, and smiled, and I smiled back,
Knowing my answer quickly would be found,
And so it was. We started, you for vac,
Me on my sentimental journey, bound
Three hours further, a nostalgic track

Both of us shared, from breakfast time to noon,
As middle England beautifully went by
Outside the window, undulating, green,
Each of us catching one another's eye
And smiling, without words. Should I have seen
That envelope you fingered lovingly,

Inscribed "Ms. N.L. Hill, Homerton College",
Or taken in, across that crevasse-aisle
Between nineteen and fifty-two, your knowledge
Of pleasures past, each northward-speeding mile
Dimming the May Week "Footlights", as your village
Timetabled nearer? Then another smile

At Nottingham, where both of us got off
On separate errands, and again rejoined,
Aisle and two seats between us, but as if
Glad to be back. Your "Diet Tango" drained,
You registered (fair pony-tail, blue scarf
Modestly nodding) next-seat neighbours — strained

West Indian father, bright-eyed coffee child —
Murmured towards them, offered them your sweets
To suck, as though, ten miles from Chesterfield,
Sneakers and socks, jeans-jacket, creamy-white
Slacks and dark-blue mascara clothed a mild
Madonna. Then, too quickly, Beetwell Street
Bus Station, and you stepping out. You smiled

One last time up, answering my wordless wave
Of glassed-in benediction. The bus set
Off with me only, fancying some nave
You'd honour soon. That tired spire, I bet,
Straightened to see you, as I saw you, brave
And slender, standing, waiting to be met.

Wirral

(for Gillian)

Up there, the light lasts longer, by the sea.
Right round from where New Brighton ferry boats
Used to disgorge, past Perch Rock battery
To Leasowe, Meols, Hoylake and Hilbre
Island, the evening flattens out, and floats
Inch by inch slowly down into the Dee

Like a golden parachute, flaring. At low tide,
Pools gleam between hard sinuous ribs of sand
Gazed at from Caldy Hill. The western side
Of Wirral stores the sun above the dried
Receded river. Water and green land
Blend into one beyond my reach. Abide

With me, though darkness falls at his behest,
Thurstaston rocks, her Heswall, and the stone
Of fading Parkgate! What was once our best
Still is for someone, though for us the rest
Must soon be silence, when unfeeling bone
Whitens through eager hand and surging breast.

Thor's Rock

360°! It took my breath
Away, away, away, as if I'd smashed
Clean through a skylight out of living death,
Or hit the bull's-eye with a stone, that pushed

Ripple on ever-widening ripple. Such
Circumference! Such immensities of light
All round me in a perfect circle — rich
Blue with a swelling cumulus of white,

Silvered grey-blue of water, gold and green
Of summer wheat, fat trees, and heaps of hedge
In all directions spinning out the seen
Over the curved horizon, whose far edge

Pricked up a drowned Atlantis of lost names:
Moel Fammau, humpbacked Snowdon, the Great Orme
Launched like a hover-craft on watery gleams
North towards Man, north-east towards Black Combe,

The heights above the Trough of Bowland, Long-
ridge Fell, the eastward rise of Rivington Pike;
And all between and nearer — the bleached prong
Of Leasowe, Formby sandhills, sandstone spike

Of Liverpool Cathedral. Every raw
Silo, each tall impersonal estate,
Was touched like quick magnesium, made to pour
Iridescently upwards, co-create

That dome of sunlight like a huge glass bell
High above heathland rising to the point
Of Thor's Rock, and of me. Only the mile-
off hill of Heswall's seaward-sloping front

Closed in the vast periphery. The view
South-west, as ever, was the streak of lane
That slowly led from St. Bartholomew
A mile through fields to where the Wirral train

Had once run under, where an hour ago
I'd walked on ghostly ripped-up tracks to find
A girl beside the Dee. Just mud-flats now
Shone there, and on invisibly behind

That hill. The gorse pods nearly burst, I drown-
ed in summer scents, perched high on written rock,
Straining to take it in, to jot it down,
Stretched all around, and decades, decades back.

First of December

Saturday. Twenty shopping days to Christmas.
I'd not be here, by then, six floors above
Paradise Street. In the multi-storey car-park
I waited for my wife, and suddenly love

Was flowering all around. The Sally Army
Cornets and tubas breathed 'O little town
Of Bethlehem' through Liverpool; beside me
A young chap eating chips tossed odd chips down

To pigeons, flocking. Just a couple of minutes
Up in the air, by a dirty concrete wall,
Four decades on from youth. It seemed eternal
And almost as if no time had passed at all.

1895

Somewhere in Chelsea, perhaps:
Boys going home from school
(Knee-breeches, satchels, flat caps),
One of them towing a girl,
Half an eye cocked at this chap's
Tripod, and half at the tall

Stranger, on two legs like them,
He's trying to fix on a plate
At maybe four-thirty p.m.
In the middle of autumn, or late
Winter, each tree just a stem
And bare gawky branches. The date

Is history now, and yet near
Enough for our fingers to reach
Out for, and miss; for our ear
To think it could recognise speech,
Closer up; for that great standing bear
To offer, so warm to our touch,

A lost world of wonder. How high
He rears, at the end of his rope;
How calmly, as schoolboys walk by
Gawping, he holds at the slope
His long, slender staff; how his eye
Proudly refuses to stoop

Even an inch, to take in
His showman, bugle at rest,
Children, who look up and grin,
Wary despite his repressed
Muzzle. Erect, serene,
He takes no note of the pressed

Button or bulb, of the humped
Photograph-taker, or me
A century after he slumped
Down on four paws, to be
Bear again, long since dumped
With only his fur to see.

Old Haymarket, 1955

Three Goddesses in parallel — 13,
6A and 6. Their destination blinds
Say BOWRING PARK, and GILLMOSS, and BROADGREEN
In solid capitals. — One of my finds

In Wilson's, Renshaw Street, twelve days ago,
One day before my father's funeral, thirty-
four years after they stood there waiting, so
Sure of themselves two years before the city

Scrapped all its trams. They vanished in the vac
Of '57, when I'd come down from King's.
I hardly noticed, on my loftier track
To places where a lot of lesser things

Seemed more important than the loss of these
Ancient survivals, dating from the year
When I was born. Now I begin to wheeze
At fifty-three, the picture of them here

On rails long melted down, about to start
For suburbs that no longer look the same,
Accuses me of something — of a heart
Too small, perhaps, to grasp them at the time,

Inadequate to hear their passing bells
As music, maybe, or decode the clunk
And grumble of their hard prosaic wheels —
Something like that. And then they turned to junk

In sheds and salvage yards, their grooves removed,
Their troubled cobble seas calmed to cement,
The terminus where these three trams arrived
One August afternoon, and whence they went

Back to Gillmoss, Broadgreen and Bowring Park
Unbelievably empty, then just space
With an old name on, like my father, dark
Under the ground that used to be a place.

30 September 1988

'The last trains have gone'.
                        That's what I wrote
Ten years ago this month, seeing the depot's
Blank stone façade at half-past-eight or so
One Saturday morning, waiting for a new
Muffler from Midas, opposite. It seemed
Desolate, somehow; but I only meant
Passenger trains.
                    They'd gone by '69,
Before we both came back from leave, too late
To ride across the island, and too late
To catch the Furness Withy freighter line
Across the North Atlantic: that had stopped
In 1965. In '64,
When we first came, my wife had had to fly,
Carrying our son.
                         We never saw the sea,
Have never seen the land.   It's half-past-eight
Tonight, on Friday, and the really last
Train, the last freight, has crossed the island now.
Tomorrow will be Saturday again,
But half-past-eight, or half-past-nine, or -ten,
Will bring no hoot, no clang, no drag of long
Flatcars behind the houses one road down;
No blaring metal box, no glaring light
Will lumber slowly up tomorrow night
Towards Syme's Bridge to pass us standing still
Beside the level crossing, watching it go
Into the darkening west.

                              Six years ago
We moved downtown. Off sick, and in the bath,
I heard the freight trains wailing, and their wheels
Patiently clanking, twenty miles an hour,
Towards that hamlet from a Chekhov play,
That arching span, that dream at the dead end
Of a dirt road: Terra Nova.
                                   It's five days
Short of our silver wedding. Just how long
Before they rip the tracks up, and our eyes
Blur, gazing along them, out of sight,
At ghost trains, lost in Terra Incognita?

Mountains

(for Yuriko)

By semi-express it only took an hour;
A flat rice plain, five stations clicking past
Eastward to Tosu, then another eight
North into Hakata. Which meant, at last,

You, a few stops by densha, or a quick
Taxi. Why was it then, that spring, I wanted
To spin it longer? Did I need to make
The journey earn the arrival? Was I haunted

By premonitions it was fading out,
Too much too soon? Did I feel more than us
Needed surmounting, so the second bout
Would shrink the main event? Why not the bus,

Even, the green and white, that left at eight
And took till half-past noon, climbing so slow
Past the hot spring, up to the seeming-near
Nick in the range, then down to Tenjinnocho

Through interminable foothills? Did that seem
Too easy to deserve you, too much horse-power?
What I took, instead, was the all-stations train,
Wooden seats, steam: twenty minutes to Mitagawa,

Then off into the unknown on foot, a road
But soon a track, towards the wireless mast
And golf-ball of Mount Seburi, tee'd in snow
A thousand metres up. No chance. Stuck fast

In unthawed drifts the map had never shown,
I couldn't lift a foot except to turn
Backwards: not even a thirty miles below
Reconnaissance of you with which to burn

Triumphant home. Of course, it didn't work.
I caught a cold, but phoned you that I'd tried
Walking to reach you. Faintly I still hear
Surprise in your voice, but not what you replied.

Four Mile Point

Christmas of nineteen fifty-eight:
Lessons and carols. Where was I,
When from my two-years-lost estate
Under a damp East Anglian sky
Voices began to re-inflate
Belief's balloons, and make them fly?

Near Famagusta: Three Mile Point;
Expectant, eighteen hours to go
Before the time to strike my tent
And take communion in the glow
Of knowing my espousèd saint,
Irene Pratt, was doing so

Too, in St. Michael's Garrison Church.
Perhaps we smiled, but never spoke.
Listening to Percy Moffat preach,
I let my eyes roam round, and stroke
Across that gentle face, in search
Of love, and timelessness. The clock

Has ticked on thirty years. I still
Can play the record, recognise
Just who they are whose frozen skill
In speech and singing once could rise
And lift me with them; but no thrill
Can take me back to Cyprus. Where's

St. Michael's, where's Irene Pratt,
Where's Percy Moffat, and that lean
And hungry I? From date to date
All's slide and stumble, with between
A blur of numbers. Far too late
Before we fathom what they mean.

For Oscar in Easter Week

Snow all around. In front of me the light
Changes to red. I switch the radio on.
The button clicks, and Brahms's Violin
Concerto (how many years since I heard that?)
Is caught in passing, quiveringly thin,
And instantly I'm made aware you're not

Here in the car, behind me. Where's your nose
Sniffing the air outside the wound-down pane,
Or pushing coldly on my neck again,
Impatient and alert? How the time goes!
Your long red silky hair no longer flows
Out in the wind, collects the gusty rain

For me to wipe with paper. Just five years
From your last ride, and yet it seems an age
Since all that breath exhaled along the edge
Of one quick needle, all that living fur's
Glossiness faded, and the final wedge
Of excavated earth sealed down the ears

You used to flap. A part of me was spent
That day. The traffic signal turns to green,
The car obeys, and Brahms's Violin
Concerto says that lives are only lent,
Not given. Ghosted by your mouldered skin,
It is my own lost selves that I lament.

Indian Meal Line

Just down the garden, just beyond its sight,
Brought me the country. An amazing glade
Beside a stream, half sunlight, half in shade,
The purl of quiet water, and a white

Goose with an orange beak. I clambered down,
He or she waded over, and we met
Just feet apart, me sitting on a bit
Of smoother rock, the goose with sidelong frown

Settling its skirts on grass. Not big enough
To chase me off, just big enough to share
Respectful silence — bird and man aware
They weren't the same, yet in a kind of love

Existing, co-existing. For at least
Ten minutes, stretching out as though an hour,
We savoured solitude so close together,
Until it swayed serenely back, that beast

Out of a fable, leaving me a feather,
White feather upon feather in the grass,
For hands to sift, to weightlessly amass
And fill my pockets with, as soft as flour.

In Memory of Colonel Robert Shaw

His high horse seems to float.
Easy for it to bear
That concentrated, slight
Figure into the air.
He smiles with such a rare
Sweetness. The trumpet's note

Thins, and the beating drum
Muffles. He seems to shine
Like steady starlight, come
Such distance to refine
Their watching flesh, and mine,
Into pure spirit. Numb

With premonition, we
Watch as he seems to swim
Forward, as history
Carries his horse and him
Down, on its iron whim,
Towards a summer sea

Where he will drown in sand
For ever. That still face
Expresses all. His hand
Salutes with not a trace
Of irony, his grace
Blesses. We only stand

And watch him go. He fades
To nothing, disappears
In myth. His bronze upbraids
More than a hundred years
Withered, but has no ears
To hear us from the shades.

Ghosts

Indian corn on the road to Harpers Ferry
In late October, days from Hallowe'en.
We stopped, astonished, our itinerary
Suspended, as you scrambled out, so keen
To photograph what we had never seen
From any road but here. South-western Mary-
land in the Fall. Drive gently, said the sign

That led to this, a gentle morning landscape
Dipping away, then rising into hills
Of rusty grey, on every side an inscape
Unique and unsuspected. How the mills
Of God grind small, how middle-age brings thrills
Youth never knew, collected in this transcript
Of one real place, these mild and glossy stills

From somewhere else. The sound was almost silent,
A susurration underneath the breath
From field to field of maize that shook, unviolent,
Emptied of any aftermath of death
A hundred years and more ago. What saith
The Preacher — all our flesh is grass? Those brilliant
Exploding particles lay dispersed beneath

Acres of cornstalks now. Whatever battled
Was spread invisible as dust around
The arrow of that rural road, had settled
Inches by inches deeper into ground
No feet would tread but farmers' feet, who found
Tall stalks to turn to cornmeal; long-unfettled
Cavalry hooves; cold ashes, dry and browned.

Sunday Morning, Paris

'Aidez-nous, S.V.P.', it said
On the neat placard by her head,
Above the dog's. I passed her by,
Dragging my luggage, wondering why
I did, as always, nothing. Loose
Francs in my pocket, little use
Now I was leaving. They'd have bought
Something, perhaps, some life support
For either, both. They'd surely share,
She by the wall, he lying there
Black muzzle tilted to the hand
That stroked it, smiling. What a land —
Two cats, a llama, and a goat
Collecting francs, and now my throat
Caught by this simple 'Aidez-nous'
Of woman and Alsatian. Who
Could pass them by, so near the rich
Pickings of cheese and meat and fish
In Place Monge market? Would they starve
Next to God's plenty? Now I'm half
The day beyond them, guilt unwashed
By Channel water, still uncashed
A hundred francs at least. Ten pounds.
I could have spared it, given grounds
For smiling, trusting. 'Aidez-nous'.
Did someone help them? Words won't do.

The Long Valley
(for Averil)

'Riding to Angers with the morning light
Behind us, down the valley of the Loire'
I chanted to the windscreen of my car
Under my breath; but had no chance to write
The words till afternoon, or even night,
Jotted above 'At Chartres (Le Grand Monarque),

Chinon, Domaine de Puy' — our dinner wine
Smelling of violets. That was back in May,
Friday the twenty-fourth. Seven weeks less a day
Later, what hope for even one more line
To carry on what started off at nine
o'clock, leaving Saumur and underway

For further west, or furthest we could go
Before we turned from shining spits of sand
And trees and water to the hinterland
North-east and home. 'The poem would be slow
Furtively finished on the plain'? Just so.
That bottle said it, and my emptying hand.

Revisiting

Five Sundays back. Mid-morning, early June
But dull. We didn't want to go to church,
Or pore through papers till the afternoon.

'Let's go somewhere', you said. But where to search
For landscapes, fresh sensations? We were tired
From yesterday's, but couldn't bear to perch

Indoors. 'Just for a potter'. In our hired
Car, off we went, and suddenly I knew
Where I was going, where was the desired

Terminus — not so much a place, a view,
Rather a state of mind. I didn't say
Till we were headed west. 'Only a few

Miles more', I kept repeating, as the day
Turned sunnier, wider, and the growing fields
Spread green and yellow, sharp against the grey

Of Huntingdonshire skies, where flatness yields
To swoops and curves, and road-signs change their style
To simple fingers, pointing: Leighton Bromswold,

Hamerton. After that, only a mile
Really, and I was back on that thin lane
Along the ridgeway. Nothing, all the while

I hadn't been there, altered: yet again
A steeple to the left, and one in front,
And in between, first hidden, then in plain

Sight, less than a hamlet, once the haunt
Of men and women fleeing from the world,
Now that once more, but no-one there. Intent

On something else, the buildings seemed. We filled
Space with our car and silence with the slam
Of doors; but just a minute's walk unfurled

Tranquillity of susurrating trees
All round us, up from Alconbury Brook
Unseen there drifted bleatings on the breeze

Of distant lambs, the grassy hillside shook
Like a wave heaving, and the stone façade
Of Little Gidding chapel gave a look

That called us in. We'd come there by the road
One had to come there by, and from the place
One had to come from, and at last we trod

The floor that led between long face-to-face
Dark-panelled pews towards tall glass and God
Made man. In that high-barrelled pregnant space

The words of Eliot and of Herbert read
Each other in embroidery by hands
Anonymous, and living learned from dead

What, living, they could only bring to sound
Without a meaning. Ghostlily their tune
Embraced us, echoing in that hallowed ground.

Tanglewood, 1991

'Lawn tickets?' Two were pressed upon us free,
And so we only paid ten bucks to sit
Out on the lawn, behind the Shed, we three
In Happidrome. We found a spreading tree
That still had shade enough for one last bit

Of grassy ground. Our son had lugged a few
Squares of old blanket from the Chevrolet
We'd left in ranks of better cars to stew
In August Massachusetts heat. We threw
Them down, then partly perched and partly lay

Waiting for things to start. So many there —
A fair field full of culture-vulture folk,
Some boasting picnic basket, patio chair,
Table and wine; some without much to spare
Save concentration on a dime store book

Or on the branching trees above, and cloud
That maybe hinted rain out of a sky
Still summer-blue. With such a rhubarb crowd,
What hope for Beethoven to sing aloud
And break our deafness? Just how much would fly

Free of that convex open-ended tin
We couldn't see inside? And then it came,
That vibrant pianissimo, ushering in
Struggle and peace. You could have heard a pin
Drop, or a rustling leaf; until that flame

Out of the past burned upwards to consume
Invisibly the Berkshire air, and held
Two thousand in a wall-less, roofless room
Silent and still. A few would tap, and hum,
A few would come and go; but nothing spoiled

That final summer concert, and our first,
Not even the slow creak of tired old bones
Adjusting, re-adjusting. One last gust
Of music, and our pent-up bodies burst
In claps that must have undermined the stones

Of snooty Lenox. Plate on license plate
Had flocked to be a part of that applause —
New Jersey, Massachusetts, New York State,
Vermont, New Hampshire. Some would get home late
Down the Taconic. We had time to pause

And take things in: a ride from Williamstown
By hill and dale to Stockbridge; then a share
In joy, one perfect Sunday afternoon
At Tanglewood, at season's end. How soon
Before we sat once more, together, there?

Levelling

No need for a high bridge, now
                There's no railway line.
They widen the road, they bring the high bridge down.
                In a month there'll be no sign

Job's Bridge ever over-arched
                The river, the track
Where freight cars waited and shunting engines lurched.
                That span with a twisted back

Is sealed each end, and the teeth
                Of shovels and scoops
Bite into parapets, reveal beneath
                Road-stone the fossil hoops

Of nineteenth-century rusted
                Iron. Three nights ago
We felt it under our feet, not quite to be trusted,
                But braver than what, below,

Was whitely inching across
                Water and waste ground
Where a notice once said NO HUMPING. Loss
                Of the past lay all around,

But the bridge obliquely soared
                As high as the gulls
That swooped to scavenge the banks of the Waterford
                River, and we could see the hulls

On stilts in the dockyard. Soon
                We shall only creep
To the southside on a cement pontoon
                When they've made a clean sweep.

Elegy for William Mathias

You're dead in August. Fifty-seven,
The age I'll be next year. I thought,
When you retired from what you taught,
You'd just compose; but it was heaven
You went to, only briefly given
Anglesey as your sunset port.

Cancer, the paper said. I smoke
And listen to your First, your Second.
Never a Third. A finger beckoned
And something lurking in you woke
And took you out. You see the joke
By now, perhaps, divinely quickened.

The joke's on me, the cohort-peer
You never met, who wrote just books
And nothing lasting like your *Lux
Aeterna*. Now you'll never hear
That poem with your name, I fear,
Carelessly spelled. The summer clocks

Have jumped an hour, and more. Too late
To kill that reticence, to send
Word of me. At some summer's end
We'll be the same, and you can wait.
For now, I hear you through the gate,
Contemporary, stranger, friend.

Palm Sunday, Thornton

Some of those lanes seemed just to disappear.
A river stopped them, that I couldn't see —
All was so flat. Yet Easter soon to be
Whispered in breezes through the clear blue air

Over what seems in memory waving corn,
Or something golden. Just beyond Back Lane,
That was; but there's no going back again,
No chance, such years gone past, of being born

A second time, of hearing church bells ring
(If ring they did — the sound has faded now)
From Sefton, Aughton, and from Aughton Brow
Across to me, a twelve-year-old in Spring

Smelling the pussy-willows in some hedge
Just beyond reach, or half-a-mile behind,
And gazing over fields into a blind
Infinity at the horizon's edge.

Creation

'As torrents in summer', Elgar said
— Lucky Elgar, with a tune in his head —
'Suddenly rise'. Those words, in June,
Suddenly rose, and then the tune
To set them to. Or say the tune
Came first, then the miraculous phrase
They fitted. Worcestershire summer days
With torrents rising out of the ground
And words to carry them, tunes he found
Till there were none to find: no words,
No tunes, no torrents, no more birds
Flying on wings of song, no 'Man,
I've a tune in my head', the torrents gone.